JUSTICE HAS RISEN FROM DEATH A THOUSAND TIMES

by
DIANE CONRAD

Justice Has Risen From Death A Thousand Times
© 2019 Diane Conrad

All rights reserved, except in brief quotations
embodied in critique or review articles.

Any reproduction, transmission, transfer, import
or similar processes in whole or in part, either
permanently or temporarily, is against the law.

PhantasmaPress
P.O.Box 1565
Albany, OR 97321, USA
phantasmapress@q.com
phantasmapress.com

Books by PhantasmaPress via Amazon.com
Bulls Bears Dragons on Wall Street
Fables of Psyche
Zen Thunder

Table of Contents

Dedication..i
Introduction...ii

Chapter I   Pain

In This Unforgiveable..1
Sorcerers...2
Comprehend...4
Caged..5
Longer...6
Remember..8
Gaming...9
The Eatery..10
Creations..11
Black Marbles..12
Waiting Room...13

Chapter II   Ponder

To Where...17
Procession..18
Broken..20
Graveyard..21
Pauper Plates..22
Circle..23
Dreaming Through Day And Night..................................24
Awakening..26
Caught In The Middle...27

Chapter III   Passage

Ferocity Of Tears..31
Tears...32
Muse...33
Struggle..34
Benevolence..36
Our Song...37
The Devotees..38

Passing Shadows..39
Dreams...Webs Storms...40
Day's Dusk..42
Impart..43

Chapter IV   Passion

Tasting...47
J...48
It's You...49
Invitation...50
Whispers That Bond Us...51
Beauty...52
Reminiscence..53
Commonwealth..54
The Music..55
On My Way To You..56
Ready..57

Chapter V   Promise

Journey Wo/Man..61
Ever Remembered...62
Could Be..63
Our Sod..64
Opaque Spirit Of Humanity...65
Up Down...66
Glowing Gifts...67
No Down..68
Family..69
Nod And Agree..70
Wings..71

Epilogue..72

DEDICATION

To those who have walked
paths strewn with
rose petals and
silver thorns

INTRODUCTION

"...people of the world, busy in thought, turning their eyes towards the countless spheres that shine above us, and making them reflect the only images their minds contain....So do the shadows of our own desires stand between us and our better angels, and thus their brightness is eclipsed."
Charles Dickens

The light of this book is gleaned
from lines and partial lines
written by other authors.

Quotes on these pages are not used
to enlighten intentions of their original authors
but to symbolize the themes throughout these chapters.

The realities of injustice and inequity
shadow-dance with the poetry-speak in this book.

The citizen-voice is spoken to
those particular corporate-chieftains and oligarchs
who put financial profit above all else
who overlook morality and honor in
humanity of the Common Good.

The realities of justice and equity
rumble relentlessly throughout this book.

The citizen-heart is blended with
the steadfast heart of fairness and equality
throbbing uneclipsed by words
more loud than the growl of plutocracy.

Truth spoken to power---**Compassion can eclipse greed**.

CHAPTER I   PAIN

IN THIS UNFORGIVEABLE

"Like a corpse on a thawing river…"
    Anna Akhmatova

our lives float and freeze on the slime of injustice
uncertain carriage to nowhere
inequity haunts every shoreline on which
corporate-chieftains want us to stand and
clap at the sounds of their clanking coins
as they ferry pass our shore of sorrow

carnage by corporate greed has crept silently
deep into our empty blanched bones
our mouths voiceless   our hopes disfranchised

victims in undertow do not
celebrate conquest over
ourselves   our brothers   our sisters
nor do we hail those whose
blind opulence admires itself
in frozen mirrors hiding
their own cracks

justice lies stiff beside us
in our icy watery graves

despair is our shroud

SORCERERS

"...seek to alchemize one's profligate sins into virtue."
Ta-Nehisi Coates

cold-blooded oligarchs
primp and prance
in cracked mirrors
beauty imagined

cold greed fires veins
for personal prosperity
no matter inequity
blood into gold imagined

cold envelops our chest
invades our lungs
we stand in wind
breathing frigid air

cold inundates our flesh
quiver as a way of life
squeezes blood vessels impotent
we shiver for shelter

in this frigid
all we ask is
shelter from corporates'
bitter air and icy glare

mercy should never
be questioned

oh Spirit to warm our inners
bring peace to
hair-follicles standing tall
in soldier rigidity
over our bristled bodies

freon rains from colorless sky
intermixes with tears on our cheeks
eyes and souls drowning
we cannot see our dreams

corporate-chieftains scroogely alchemize
profit into fallacious grace

standing in witness
we know the truth

frozen crystals of their cold greed
cannot spark warmth

COMPREHEND

*"...understand why my heart
 does not beat faster under your hand."*
Anna Akhmatova

as if using a potter's spinning wheel
oligarchs' slight-of-hand molds trickery
from the cold wet clay of plutocracy

as if on the wheel of their spinning avarice
we run round and round through
the gray sludge of their greed

our legs slip and grope for next steps
anguish contours our every stride
our hearts are stilled under their sculpt

chiseled and cast by inequity
we cannot be our own artisans
we are lost in loss

CAGED

*"Why did you turn the last freedom
 Into a den of thieves?"
    Anna Akhmatova*

cold fog rises
off these rock walls
misty water
clings to chilled skin
eerie air pervades
this cavern of mystery
freedom obscured

as we toil exhausted   voiceless
in this enigma
it is phantom crimes
by which robbers at our backs
claim stakes to labor not their own

to corporates' lair of lies
of promise for golden cage
we listen to their murky prattle
which babbles louder than
any songbird's freedom

we cannot escape their deafening deceit
which robs our every song

through the dark darkness
our own shadows creep before us

an unseen wind howls   *pain*

our arms are not wings

LONGER

"...receiving, taking, hoarding and marketing features of our political economy that shrink us backward into death."
Charles Hampden-Turner

longer than one election cycle
inequity piles brick on brick
builds this solid maze
we are encased

    we are enchained while avarice politicos
    swagger in opulence begotten by
    injustice wheeled by their own
    conniving plutocracy

longer than one moment in history
these shameless slimy putrefied
demons of immoral greed
strut inequity

    permeated with corporate's darkness
    our dark bones slip on the path
    of flaming despair on which
    we Have-Nots stumble

longer than righteous laugh louder than our tears
willful ignorance of their own shameless greed
encumbers corporateers to know how
to ask for forgiveness

    in our exhaustive crawling over
    hideous obstacles of injustice
    we will not creep into our
    own graves passively

longer than our suffering
our deaths will not be
their salvation
from greed

REMEMBER

"And which disaster is the shadow of the other?"
Anna Akhmatova

oligarchs churn our lives into
not enough   not enough   not enough
the reverie of every day

under which star is anyone born

lamentfull dreams harden these bones
by which we strain to stand erect
we raise our thin fingers not
to hail ravenous juntas but
to point to their shrinking humanity

what does their corporate
carnivorous cupidity serve

are not our sobs enough praise

this mammoth tide of greed
will eventually recede into
our ocean of sweat and tears
and reveal every grain of
humanity once drowned
by their avarice

under the shadow of truth
their souls will shrivel in
what they remember some night

GAMING

"Where life is not a breath..."
James Montgomery

in this game of life
behind closed corporate doors
money-wheels spin in high-stake contests
players with fingers dressed in diamonds
excitement round and round
gears and cheers

our own fingers bleed
touching cogs whirling
out of our control
in oligarchs' tyrannical
greed-game

with each spin we sense
the passage of our youth
turning turning into
a lifetime of have-not

our eyes squint watching these neon wheels
we stand blinded   stunned   breathless
our red hands and empty pockets
fill a vacuum life

our life of chance
has no chance
equity lost

THE EATERY

"To be grown up is to sit at the table with people who have died..."
                    Edna St Vincent Millay

like beasts devouring meat
on bones of the Unsuspecting
avarice juntas ravage the Every-Wo/man
their money concocts the receipts

corporate cooks hurriedly set the table
no chairs for anyone to sit
at name-plates for
Compassion   Liberty   Equity   Justice

corporate fingers grab
drumsticks and gizzards
stuff their mouths with lies
bloat their bellies with greed
vomit all truth of fair game

only after plates are laid before us
do we notice who is missing at the table
only after being served do we realize
table manners are a game within a game and
starvation is our hidden prize

only when grown-up can we leave the table
moneylicious   not our taste
we leave no tip for gluttony the umpire
at juntas' table games
held in funeral parlors

CREATIONS

"You do not have enough misery so you create more."
Victor Hugo

beginning each day
we enter history

look back to
look forward

what is seen
will be seen

heritage in
abiding evolution

wretchedness rejuvenates

lustful corporations
echo ravage

enough is
never enough

shrill on shrill
exponentially

more is
never fulfilled

misery is
never singular

BLACK MARBLES

"Marble crumbles away. Everything is on the verge of death."
Anna Akhmatova

like black marbles cascading
down the hill of humanity
corporate-chieftains make
rubble of every courthouse
leave nothing of fair value

black marbles lay
a slippery slope on which
subjugated sojourners struggle
to not stumble in despair
to not lose solid foundation of
justice for all

every wo/man
dressed in dust and
shoes of patched soles
wobble with every step
on menacing path cannot
advance beyond this present
impoverished inherited journey
every route dismal with trickery of
corporates' black marbles underfoot
stay alive   stay alive   is our staggered chant

we are given a handful of black marbles
as offering for equity but
our hands are full of empty

thank you
drowns in our tears

WAITING ROOM

"My silence can be heard everywhere
 It fills the courtroom"
   Anna Akhmatova

corporate indifference shouts
praise for injustice
we do not hear as our own

we listen in silence
in darkness
empty

heavy stillness
no breath whispering
justice

we are black shadows on black walls
black on black overwhelms the room
we languish in fear of pending destitution
fragile existence suffered

corporateers as black statues on benches
sit stricken in fear of the verdict
guilty-as-sin
apprehensive existence endured

filled is this room
brimmed with hush

trial of waiting as mid-wife
equity not yet born

CHAPTER II   PONDER

TO WHERE

"You led me where there were no roads"
Anna Akhmatova

as toddlers
the world is a safari
we crawl with curiosity
exploration is our happy
no need for specified paths
destinations are everywhere
wonder abounds

as adolescents
the world is a challenge
every choice leads to doubt
every where leads to destitute
oligarchs selfishly plot a barren landscape
our search for guideposts is achingly thwarted
friendless abounds

as adults
the world is a wasteland
we become pauper and wanderer
walk on dirt covered with empty pockets
no compass   no clan   no stars for guidance
no place to flourish in compassionate community
futility abounds

Where do oligarchs travel to celebrate humanity?

PROCESSION

"Walking…
And behind us there are millions like us
And never was a procession more hushed"
                    Anna Akhmatova

millions of dry throats choke
breathlessly mutter
truth to power

millions of blistered feet stomp on
grounds of immoral apathy
mud sucks worn shoes
in ditches of despair

in freedom's march millions of shoulders
press side by side quietly throng to
hope's rise for equity

in what time will these millions

without loss   grief   tears dripping
without blame   shame   faces hiding

dare reject status quo
dare hear progressive's call
dare transform today's prejudice

without insult   speak
without assault   touch
without blindness   look
without judgment   embrace

in what time will these millions

with the voice of truth   courage   pride
unleash the hush which is deafening

Can tomorrow's justice nobly
shout and parade beyond
today's plutocracy?

BROKEN

"The gazes of love are stained with tears"
Anna Akhmatova

thick scarlet blood
falling

no empathy to hear
the splash

upon the surface of
this wanton world

emotions ripped
hearts dissected

flailing hope gropes
for connection

eyes gaze through copious tears
in desire for compassion

Will broken hearts
beat tomorrow?

Will oligarchs look back
with woeful regret?

Will hollow greed echo
its own pompous pain?

GRAVEYARD

"Have blood to spurt upon the oppressor's hand."
Edna St Vincent Millay

juntas' fat hands full of felony
hold sharp steel swords pointed
at our oppressed hearts

our own haggard hands empty
bleed across their blade of inequity
our blood dripping endlessly

Can our red wet fingers grip
the shovel of justice and
bury our own undertakers?

PAUPER PLATES

"Why did you poison the water
And mix dirt with my bread?"
Anna Akhmatova

in a country where cupboards were full throughout the land
in a time when justice was the rule of citizens
it is now more than unfathomable
to stand witness to unfettered
greed and the silence of
stealth oppression
plutocracy

our veins woefully parch as blood pours
onto stones of corporate indifference
our mouths are opened wide silent
our stomachs cramp with empty
our skeletons rattle in thirst
we lie in paupers' beds
stiff   cold   hungry

Will equity ever grace our plates?

CIRCLE

"Why then are you circling like a thief"
Anna Akhmatova

in cycles

clouds form mountains

water bathes earth

light reveals truth

compassion begets community

love engenders justice

never-the-less

life holds mystery
Why is your life a labyrinth?

darkness cloaks choice
Why does your compass point to greed?

money barters influence
Why do you claw at purse strings?

sand shifts uncertainty
Why do you live in castles of coin?

oligarchs steal shamelessly
Why do you circle plutocracy?

DREAMING THROUGH NIGHT AND DAY

"Through darkness like a falling star."
  Anna Akhmatova

daylight scopes the rubble of decayed neglect
children waste as condemned orphans
parents sob for bereft procreation
flowers fallow on vacant land
inspirations barren
visions vagrant

hazed sun imprints wandering lonely shadows
eclipse of heart suffered from dawn to dusk
breath of vibrant life stifled
no soulful satisfaction
no potent promise
impotence

night-breezes brush aimlessly across barren soil
birds labor on heavy wings in vacant sky
sunset descends moaning into void
mountains wait in stillness
pain heartfelt while
time searches for
justice

hazed moon imprints wandering lonely shadows
eclipse of heart suffered nightly
breath of vibrant life stifled
no soulful satisfaction
no sweet surrender
into peaceful
slumber

escape into sleep an illusion searching for truth
surreal clowns clap inside our dreams
laugh loudly at aspirations
for equitable laws
unwritten

truth of despair and torment dominate
our flimsy phantom fantasies of
dream-secrets for democracy
crying aloud
unheard

nightmarish inequity mocks
any promise for
restful soul

Will wakefulness survive
this dark?

AWAKENING

"...in dreams is most awake."
Coventry Patmore

down-cast down-trodden
darkness is our precept
we learn the book of
despair

this life of forsaken is not alive
caught in dismal slumber
eyes shuttered we are mired
injustice sucks us down
into the muck of nightfall
we toss and turn   our hands grope
searching blindly for beyond torment
dejection

oh to toss off this blanket of inequity
so intrusively taring our dreams
for fresh morning rise
oh let us not be darkly mesmerized
discouraged

How awakening would it be
to have dreams enliven our days with
smiles at equity's call?

CAUGHT IN THE MIDDLE

"As the future ripens in the past
So the past rots in the future"
*   Anna Akhmatova*

in the middle of heartbeats
caught between
anxiety   confusion
juxtaposed in
pause   promise   pump
      inhale

in the middle of heartbeats
caught between
present hush and
future bloodrush
hesitation interjects
      doubt

in the middle of heartbeats
tension   wonder
brief rest for reflection
humanity stilled
      anticipation

the cycle of today-tomorrow
is confiscated by the evermore

time's pledge is   hope
time's fool is   greed

Will our heartfelt saga survive
to witness justice in perpetuity?

CHAPTER III   PASSAGE

FEROCITY OF TEARS

"To the point of tears...in our dreams."
Anna Akhmatova

in our dreams
hearts are not still
unicorns prance for joy
no bridles to control freedom

in our dreams
tears are not silent
their ferocity slackens
the grip of avarice juntas

our tears one at a time
drown the agony of injustice

our impassioned eyes
brighten with equity's glow

we gladly shed tears of faith

TEARS

"...where tears live..."
  Anna Akhmatova

yearning
we valiantly raise our open eyes
toward a brave path to liberty
hopeful faces glimmer
forlorn mood wanes
weeping tears dry

knowing
equity is held in memory
plutocracy cannot obliterate
our organic craving for justice
the shadow of justice-past haunts
its own necessity in our vagabond lives

wo/men do not live
to only tearfully grieve

children will learn to play more than
a game of funeral

MUSE

"But let me not be on earth to witness
The golden stamp of failure"
  Anna Akhmatova

fall of snow   sway of flowers   frolic of leaves   force of wind
play of unseen gusts hold unpredictable lift
shadows dance as sun ascends   descends
earth turns through its own history

mankind womankind
born into childhood nescient
students of the unknown
foreigners to self   sky

how can anyone fathom cycles of life
winter into yet another spring
the stirs of joy   hope   èlan
the promise for each season's gift of equal rights

let not our breaths stop until
the golden age of reason is
witnessed for all time

let us not wander this earth aimlessly
we are not shameful sheep

STRUGGLE

"For this morose beast within my breast   To become a heart."
                    Anna Akhmatova

we race back and forth in life's abyss
we toss ourselves into the swirl of mortality
we let bloods mix   mesh
we feel throbs of gruesome   awesome

desire   congeals
brilliance   clabbers
conscience   curdles

oh to the Sisyphus within us

we race up and down in hope's chasm
we toss ourselves into the swirl of humanity
we grapple in our dreams
we strain to snare illusive justice

sullen souls   contort
opaque paragons   confound
the unfathom   cascades

oh to the farce within us

jesters dance on people's rights
laugh at their own conniving jokes
sing songs like those sung over tombstones
empathy not yet beating in their jokester hearts

we open wide
our tearful eyes
our yearning hearts

our tongues scream
hope is life's truth
plutocracy is life's lie

oh to the throb within us

bones of justice are inner strength
our skeletons swing in winds of change

we live greater than
the life in which we are born

BENEVOLENCE

"Torment proved to be my muse..."
       Anna Akhmatova

if you were honest
    we would listen
if you were fair
    we would approach
if you were lawful
    we would heed

as it is
    we stand up to endure your trickery
    we will not be ruled by fraud

because you are greedy
    we shun you
because you are villainous
    we denounce you
because you are shameful
    we look above you

as it is
    we stare down ominous plutocracy
    we will not be ruled by menace

as it has proved to be
    we raise our hands for humanity
    we embrace heroism for the Common Good
    we sing devotional songs in harmonized benevolence

OUR SONG

"We come with nothing more than the voice of truth and reality."
Anna Akhmatova

choked by fat fingers of hands
which raid the tills of our dreams
muted throats are
the stifle of every day

snug out of sight hiding
corporate cashiers smirk while
leaving askew their tray of
inequitable laws

the sound of dirge
fills our coffers while
our empty hearts are heavy

greed grinningly clangs its own call
the ring of coins' count deafens
any sound of truth

with little more than a song of faith
we come now as messages
with proud voices chanting

intrepid future ever tolls
the destiny by stronger voices
calling truth   howling reality
oligarchs shame!   oligarchs shame!

THE DEVOTEES

"And the voices of invisible speakers resound."
        Anna Akhmatova

heads droop   shoulders hunch
burdens carried in solitude cause despair
we cannot stand alone in darkness

we can walk each step together
with feet steady on this
trampled ground trodden by
ragged boots of our legendary hunters
who searched for more than existence as
specks of proletariat
let our own march and voice resound also

we can believe in each other
from parents to children
as comrade-in-arms

whoever you are and have been
we listen to your words of witness
to every rape of humanity

your presence lingers throughout generations
your compassionate voice is a canopy of hope
you captivate our desire for justice
you enlighten our soul for equity
we are enriched by your embrace of
compassionate community
beloved democracy

PASSING SHADOWS

"there is this edge where shadows
and bones of some of us
walk backwards"
      Joy Harjo

fear inundates
    stagnant in black shadows
    our thin frail bones
    cower beneath our shoulders
    powerless to move
    we crouch in darkness

pride engulfs
    avarice ambition gleefully
    unleashes corporate greed
    whips equity in its path
    cloaks light of justice
    embraces darkness

juntas convulse
    ambushed by money-lust
    look for evermore gratification
    blindly grasp for praise
    drown in their own
    darkness

roles of victims intertwist

    someday may we all
    be born twice but
    let there be no echo
    of our birth-cries

DREAMS---WEBS---STORMS

"We didn't know until the end,
What to call one another."
     Anna Akhmatova

dream-beings in unison to dream-beat
magical dance in magical world
twirl in deception
reality of little value

life   a strand of silken spider-string
weaves webbed patterns
delicate and un-embraceable
magical existence

the unpredictable lattice of daily life
does not display its final design
surprise can appear
in dark fibers

in the complex web-of-greed
equity will be snared and
death will come slowly for innocents
entangled in weaved patterns of deceit

corporate-chieftains   weavers and thunder-makers
noise and rain   their loom
hurricanes   their dream of strength

our feet splash in their torrent mud but
our souls braid as one fabric unsoiled
our dreams of affirmation will not be drenched
we will never drown in their ominous storms

their thunder-bolts fling bright white
awaken us from a life of nocturnal spindling
every wo/man looks up
lightning's flair lights our vision of
strong and embraceable justice

like wings of eagles full of vigor and rainbow
we stroke and weave in our own emblazoned skies
our vision outshines the gray tempest
hurled by oligarchs' thunder of greed

mysterious partnerships
reality---dreams
life---webs
storms---rainbows
lightening---vision

Friend---Foe

DAY'S DUSK

"The one now in gloom tomorrow will bloom."
Anna Akhmatova

in this sultry twilight
comrades embrace in heartfelt exchange
human whispers softer than crickets'
tell tales of this day's struggle to be
free from the black claw of greed

soft crimson spreads gently overhead
sun quietly joins silver sea
water becomes cool steel
sky slowly gracefully grays
air sighs with day's end

in the dusk of reminiscence
we sit calmly shoulder to shoulder
eyes close in hushed anticipation of
tomorrow's valiant march for
truth-to-power

IMPART

"Imparting, in its glad embrace
Beauty to beauty, grace to grace!"
   John Greenleaf Whitier

from dust to devotion

  in the wake of loneliness
         embrace

  in the wake of embrace
         kinship

  in the wake of kinship
         compassion

  in the wake of compassion
         community

from hollow to echo

CHAPTER IV   PASSION

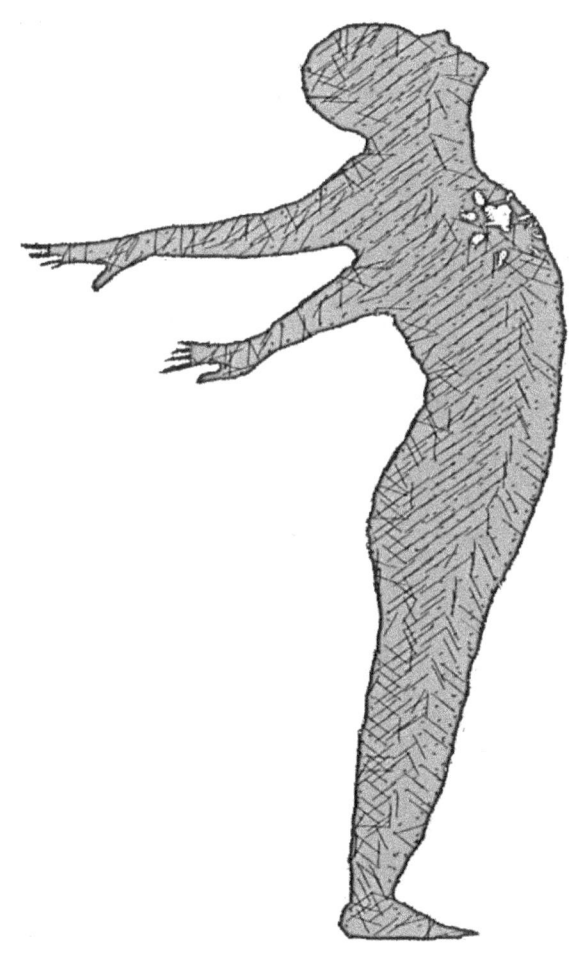

TASTING

tasteful   intoxicating
tantalizing bouquet of
peaceful freedom
abundant equity

the ambrosia of justice
ferments in mature charm
tongues will taste a flavor
other than common greed

as corporateers raise their glasses
I give this toast

be gentle with my body
my skin might steam

be gentle with my mind
my thoughts might scream

be gentle with my feelings
my tears might stream

be gentle be gentle
vineyards hoed with compassion
will yield an aged vintage
generations can savor with honor

generosity will be
its own harvest

J

inane air drifts by my face
I inhale the emptiness
world vacant
                                    without you

colors swish by my somber eyes
alluring hues fanciful   yet
tears come readily
                                    without you

time ticks   my heart beats   yet
happiness is only illusion
hope is elusive
                                    without you

my field of gravity is far askew
from earth's core   I pretend
to live a life resolved   yet
                                    absent justice haunts

my bleak inner-being wrenches
your ghost fills my gut   yet
I am hollow
                                    without justice

IT'S YOU

every day much to do
to sorely survive
loving you

touch this world without your caress
sooth the sadness of your absence
cling to the truth in your heart

a hint of

justice is all I have to continue
treading with feet weary
on forsaken streets

hope for

strength to endure this daily trek
find a path to stand in witness
and shout truth to power

loving you is much to do but
to do without is beyond
my soul

you   Equity   it's you

INVITATION

I invite you into my day
spend time to be near
rest your heard on my shoulder
pause to romanticize together
let imaginations waltz in unison

let the stir of spring be close
its breath bloom wild
if the spirit of rebirth enlivens you
then I invite you into
the marrow of my bones

let me
taste the spices in your heart
smell the scent of your heat
hear the truth in your mind
see the colors in your smile   tears   skin
feel the breath of your culture

we can rise together in community
build consensus for Common Good
create ubiquitous equity

WHISPERS THAT BOND US

amid all the deafening shouts of injustice
will you come with me and whisper

together look at   and whisper
mystery in rainbows   *intrigue*
delicacy of flowers   *allure*
curves in circles   *satisfy*

together listen to   and whisper
music in birds' laughter   *harmonize*
crackle of campfire   *glow*
sway of seasons   *inspire*

together feel   and whisper
sunbeams and moonshadows   *amaze*
raindrops and oceanwaves   *marvel*
feathers and breezes   *glide*

together   whisper
sit before a sunset   *contemplate*
run toward a sunrise   *energize*
sing songs   cry tears   *animate*

together   whisper
leave plutocracy behind   *proceed*
cherish compassion   *caress*
bond in humanity   *love*

BEAUTY

strange as an unsolved mystery
charming as a shameless rose
diverse as love's gleam

hands extending help
voices bidding hope
eyes gleaming *yes*

to befriend   to cherish   to respect

thoughts of justice ever whirl through
windmills turning in my mind
enticing Venus smiles

equity's fire burns eternally
plutocracy extinguished
endearment sparked

the necessity of benevolence inspires
our humane community to call
justice for all

compassionate comradery   ageless beauty

REMINISCENCE

you come to me in
sway of wind-chimes
notions of spring sprouting
dreams of friends singing in full voices

my mind gleefully wanders
through reminiscence of your
compassion and spirited delight in
promise of determined freedom for all

more than mere imagination
you have engendered significance
to endure the heart-wrenching darkness in
uncaring brethren who lift their torch of deceit

because of you
ONWARD   is the mode of our lives
our mirrors reflect tomorrow's blessings
for the truth that all people are created equal

our restless blood
decants your name
again again   Equity Equity
worthy of resounding resonance

COMMONWEALTH

in dreams and schemes
of life's enchantment
bonding isn't hard to do
it is the force that holds me   to you

the charm of joy
courage of pain
pound of heart
spark of soul   embracing

corporates and citizens
arm in arm
in Common Cause
bewitched   together

life without community
is breath without air   truth be told

THE MUSIC

wondrous kindred tempo-vibrations
alluring rapture gently sways and swirls
I am never forsaken when musical sounds
orchestrate compassion in your warm comradery

oh player of tunes
a rainbowed harlequin
harmonizing with equity
beat after beat drumming in my core

in the inner chambers of my heart
                                   deep
                                     you sing

in my blood like a ribbon unleashed
                                   deep
                                     you twirl

as my red throbbing pulse pounds
                                   deep
                                     you dance

our melody   justice

ON MY WAY TO YOU

flights in burning passion
like a moth to land on flames
drawn by promise of flicker
yearning for light and justice

flutter-existence
on my way to you

your fire stills my breath
my body's rhythm rushes
to the heat of your flame
to be consumed completely

justice explodes in consummation

compassionate community at journey's end

READY

in a field of Van Gogh grass
a pinto stallion statuesque
poised on horizon's edge
ready to gallop onto
the green blades of justice

hold the sigh
let the moment rise in you
mount the promise

CHAPTER V   PROMISE

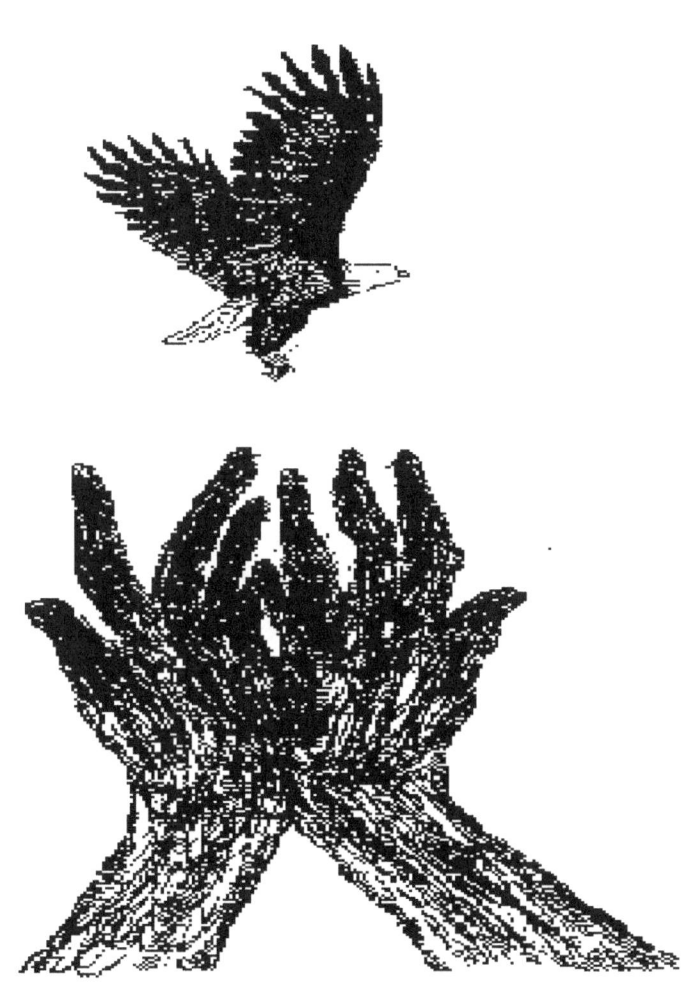

JOURNEY-WO/MEN

"He knew the details of the journey he had never taken."
Ron Sadler

we know
      flare of red desire
      anguish of steel pain
      flimsy of gossamer hope

we learn
      to participate
      to communicate
      to study the abyss

our inner wisdom
      breathes anticipation
      navigates anxiety   fear
      aspires truth   joy   justice

our journey is inherent
      past generations point
      the path on which we step
      we know our unfolding future

courage   our destination

EVER REMEMBERED

"It smells of burning."
  Anna Akhmatova

in a black box cluttered with muzzles and chains
our fingers feverously feel through darkness
we search with anticipation as
belief in equity is not lost

justice is not beyond memory
its flame brightens its own urgency
forget cannot delete
the organic necessity of fairness
it is more than a memento
to be tucked away in oblivion

we explore eagerly
warm our hearts in comradery
tell tales of the birth of freedom

our conviction in equity
enlivens more than one
instant flicker of faith

compassion burns brilliantly

COULD BE

"Everything could be redeemed and repaired."
Anna Akhmatova

if I am troubled would you listen
if I am sad would you sing a tender song
if I am distressed would you stand with me

plutocracy does not gratify those who starve
its rule of wealth is greed
 anguish brews as vinegar foams in our mouths
  discontent ferments in our flattened daily bread
   juntas' avarice does not leaven our future
    starvation is not our vision

more redeeming than a banquet fit for pigs
are the nourishments of
 moments in awakened fellowship
  spirituality in daily compassion
   inherent grace in communal soul
    harmony in wholeness beyond self

in reparation for aristocrat gluttony
our commonwealth must be balanced
on the scale of justice
salvation is our vision

children should play freely in fields of corn

OUR SOD

"A transparent shroud lies
On the fresh sod and imperceptibly melts."
Anna Akhmatova

today
the shatter of our brittle bones is deafening
the petals of your rose has sparkle thorns
your wealth and greed prick our marrow
our days are pierced by scaring grief
we are mourners in dirt fields

tomorrow
torment will be seen as a regretful ghost
imperceptible change will emerge
oligarchs with sorrowful eyes
will look longingly for
the Common Good

forever
in full sun let us all rise from fallow
to till the road of redemption

OPAQUE SPIRIT OF HUMANITY

"I should have been on my way long ago, I was only waiting for you."
Anna Akhmatova

miracles have yet to begin
harmony has yet to unfold
blessings have yet to be shared
oligarchs have yet to learn mercy
their humanity has yet to be born
our sorrow for them has yet to be still

in the should-be

miracles begin
      colors call   shapes siren
      flamboyant conversation
harmony is the theme
      alive is the music
      kinship is the revival
blessings in community
      abiding grace
      glowing hope
on sun-lit cozy days
      encircling air
      cocoons us

what should be   will be

waiting through life's inevitable passage
compassion will be born
there will be no more crucifixions

UP DOWN

"There's lots of happiness in store
For you who's free"
  Anna Akhmatova

they hover aloft
dreamscapes above our heads
entice our attention and imagination
transformations of delight
elusive untouchable substance
these clouds

in dark damp places
acaulis gently soothe stones
spread lush blankets over soil
puff green cushions under foot
create a quiet tender forest
these mosses

in this up-down world
we muse and move
through heaven and earth
we absorb diversities found
looking up
looking down

community everywhere
evokes a freedom of smiles

GLOWING GIFTS

*"When I was young, every day was a beginning of some new thing,
and every evening ended with the glow of next day's dawn."*
Iglulik Ivaluarjuk, elder

for each other

the smell of clean air
    to imbue our lungs
the sound of clear ocean
    to surround our ears
the glad greetings to all species
    to occupy our hours
the heartfelt trust in abiding equity
    to penetrate our minds
the comradery of diverse skins and ideas
    to assimilate our being

for each day's dawn

NO DOWN

"Ain't No Grave Can Hold My Body Down"
Traditional American Gospel

everyone move'n through time
one tick-tock follow'n next
ain't no stop'n as long as
we keep on keep'n on
raise'n our heads high
keep on keep'n on
praise'n our hands high
keep on keep'n on
while head'n for justice
there ain't no failure

ain't it so children
we are echoes of ourselves

FAMILY

"Inside me still, like a song or like grief..."
Anna Akhmatova

in sorrow or song we
search for whom
to admire

we offer our heart in extended hand
with hope you feel its warm pulse
joining I-You   into We

let us

expose aged dark secrets of despair
share cherished stories of smiles
show insecure selves of fear

search into amorous eyes of respect
listen to telling tongues of honor
muse in mysteries of hope

foster ardent moments of fondness
nurture embers of kinship
breed sense of family

we are all related
in hell or heaven
kindred spirits

NOD AND AGREE

"...firefly winking..."
  Jake Adam York

gossamer shadows
shade this world a mellow mood
twinkle orange   twilight lime
moral beams bounce on hope

fireflies blink dozily
tenderness lightens
the gray reality of
callous inequity

in this scene of glinting eyes
thoughts of country founded on
dignity   honor   truth   respect
take flight into democracy

sky lit only by
the light of fireflies
no wars nor distrust
comradery bursting in air

wings of vision
nod in unison
agree to declare
these precious beliefs

"We The People...
in Order to form a
more perfect Union,
establish Justice,
insure domestic Tranquility..."

WINGS

"I shall die, but that is all that I shall do for death."
Edna St Vincent Millay

during this anguished life
we have died a thousand times and a thousand times more
but in our final death we shall not die in darkness
we shall rise from the splatter of blood and the quintessence of dust
we shall pull out the silver-thorns of tarnish-inequity
our bodies will heal from Judas-plutocracy
our eyes will sparkle with forward thrust
equity will guide our winged souls up into the Common Good
and will give soar beyond past suffered injustices

our wings undeniable
                       every wingblade strong
                                          every wingtip stretched
freedom under wings
                  in sovereign flight
                                  unfettered

corporate-chieftains will crouch under
our talons which grip and carry all brethren
without judgment

beyond dying we all metamorphose into Freesouls
we shall be the power of truth
we will forevermore bay at the sun

hy ya ya   hy ya ya   equity   equity

EPILOGUE

the entrails of greed will eventually decay
in the ground and be compost for
the rise of democracy

death
gives significance to
life

everyone
will be buried
in the same Earth

www.ingramcontent.com/pod-product-compliance
Lightning Source LLC
Chambersburg PA
CBHW081452220526
45466CB00008B/2609